How a Woman Startup Founder Survives

In a Male-Dominated Business World

Copyright © 2024 Victoria Duff
All rights reserved.

Please note that *How a Woman Startup Founder Survives* is an extended copy of *The Startup Within*. The extended copy contains the same copy as *The Startup Within* but adds additional copy that relates solely to women entering the startup world and adds approximately 30% additional material.

In shadowed halls where doubt and whispers loom,
She dares to dream, her vision burning bright.
Through storms of naysayers, she finds her bloom,
Transforming trials into her guiding light.

The path is steep, with obstacles in place,
Each barrier built to guard an old regime.
But with her courage etched upon her face,
She carves new ways to realize her dream.

The glass above may shimmer, strong and cold,
Yet cracks appear with every step she takes.
Her story, one of grit and courage bold,
A testament to all the change she makes.

Through strength and will, her triumph is her own,
A founder's crown, her legacy well sown.

Contents

Contents

Introduction

Chapter 1: Introduction: Breaking Barriers, Building Dreams

Chapter 2: Personal Qualities of Failed Entrepreneurs

    Lack of Passion and Drive

    Accepting Stereotypes as Truth

    Overly Self-Critical

    Avoiding Conflict

    Reluctance to Self-Promote

    Underestimating Financial Worth

    Poor Decision-Making Skills

    Inability to Adapt

    Poor Financial Management

    Lack of People Skills

    Arrogance and Ego

    Procrastination

Chapter 3: Personal Qualities of Successful Entrepreneurs

    Professional Behavior

    Confidence in Breaking the Mold

    Patience in the Face of Bias

    Strategic Relationship Building

Clear Boundry Setting
　　Advocacy for Women in Business
　　Passion and Drive
　　Teachability
　　Resilience
　　Risk Tolerance
　　Adaptability
　　Creativity and Innovation
　　Strong Work Ethic
　　Leadership Skills
　　Effective Communication
　　Financial Acumen
　　Self-Belief
　　Unapologetic Ambition
　　The Big Picture
Chapter 4: From Idea to Launch
　　The Idea: The Foundation of Your Business
　　Market Fit: Will They Actually Pay for This?
　　Production: From Prototype to Product
　　Funding: Fuel for the Startup Engine
　　Networking: Turning Connections into Opportunities
　　Build-Out: Making a Game Plan
　　Legal: Setting Up Your Business Right
　　Accounting: Show Me the Money Management

    Compliance: Navigating the Red Tape
    Putting It All Together
Chapter 5: Advice
    Navigating the Double Standards
    Finding Allies (and Advocates)
    Reclaiming Confidence
    Changing the Narrative
    Forget the Stories of Overnight Wealth
    Don't Go It Alone
    Seek Out Advisors (Yes, Even Your Uncle Joe)
    Save Up—You'll Need It
    Consider a Startup Accelerator
    Get Ready for Rejection (Lots of It)
    Embrace a Lean Mindset
    Keep Learning and Adapting
    Final Thoughts: The Real Work Begins Now
Conclusion: The Journey Ahead
References
About the Author
    Meet Victoria Duff:

Introduction

In the mid-1970s, I became one of the first women executives in top-tier Wall Street institutional investment banking and corporate finance. Some of my male colleagues deeply resented me, but my hat is off to the few who fought for me. Just surviving required my best performance and constant strategic evaluation of the system I was working in. That is why I wrote this book.

After two decades of swimming in the shark-filled waters of Wall Street, weathering the thrills and spills of institutional bond trading desks and investment banking, I decided I'd had my fill of high-stakes stress and corporate competition. So I did what any sensible person might do after such an experience: I walked away and founded my own startup consultancy, aBusinessPlan.com. It was a leap into a world where, instead of advising Fortune 500 companies, I would find myself navigating the fascinating—and at times, utterly baffling—world of would-be entrepreneurs. Thirty years later, I've come to know this crowd like an old friend, albeit a somewhat unpredictable one. I've seen it all. The wild-eyed dreamers. The spreadsheet warriors. The "just-one-more-pitch-deck" perfectionists. And, of course, the rare breed with the grit and vision to turn their ideas into something real.

Now, when it comes to aspiring entrepreneurs, I'll admit I've developed a bit of a sixth sense. I can tell, with unnerving accuracy, who's likely to find success and who's on the express train to Disaster-ville, complete with round-trip tickets. In Chapter Two, I'll dive into the telltale signs of the latter—a category comprising some of my least favorite clients. Don't get me wrong, they're lovely people, most of them. They just tend to be as stubborn as they are starry-eyed, and no matter how hard I try to throw them a lifeline, they seem hell-bent on tangling themselves up in it. These folks are the reason I've become an expert at eyeing the warning signs of startup failure from miles away.

But then, every now and then, there's a client who makes it all worthwhile. These are the entrepreneurs who appear in Chapter Three—the rare few who not only wrangle funding but go on to build solid companies and (gasp!) actually turn a profit. They are, without a doubt, an elusive breed. So, you see, that's why I want to peel back the curtain on the brutal realities of startup life, help aspiring women founders spot their own foibles before they're knee-deep in debt, and offer a clear-eyed look at what separates the wild-eyed dreamers from the few who actually make it. From spotting a genuinely fundable idea to building a company that doesn't just survive but thrives, this book aims to arm wannabe women entrepreneurs with a clear, hard-won path through the perils ahead.

Chapter 1: Introduction: Breaking Barriers, Building Dreams

Let's start with the truth: being a woman entrepreneur is hard. Really hard. It's not just the long hours, the financial risks, or the constant need to innovate—it's also the unique, infuriating, and often invisible hurdles that come with being a woman in a business world still shaped by male-dominated traditions.

If you've ever walked into a meeting and had your intelligence questioned before you even spoke, you know what I'm talking about. If you've had to pitch an investor who seems more interested in your marital status than your revenue model, you're already familiar with the uphill battle. And if you've ever felt the crushing weight of impostor syndrome—the fear that one wrong move will "prove" what others assume about your abilities—you're not alone.

Here's the good news: while the challenges are real, so are the victories. And when women succeed, they don't just change their own lives—they redefine what's possible for everyone watching.

That's what this book is about.

Woman Startup Founder, Are You Ready for the Challenge of Female Entrepreneurship? is your brutally honest guide to navigating the chaos of entrepreneurship as a woman. It's a roadmap through the pitfalls, the setbacks, and the moments of self-doubt. But more importantly, it's a celebration of what happens when women refuse to accept the status quo, take bold risks, and build businesses that defy expectations. After all, a January, 2024 report by Wells Fargo found that from 2019 to 2023, women-owned businesses' growth rate outpaced the rate of men's 94.3% for number of firms, 252.8% for employment, and 82.0% for revenue. During the pandemic, women-owned businesses added 1.4 million jobs and $579.6 billion in revenue to the economy.

Throughout these pages, I'll shine a light on the harsh realities of startup life—especially for women. I'll unpack the traits that make successful entrepreneurs tick and the ones that spell disaster. We'll talk about the specific challenges women face in securing funding (spoiler: we get less than 3% of venture capital), the double standards we're forced to navigate, and the relentless pressure to prove ourselves in a world that's still figuring out how to value us.

But this isn't a pity party. It's a rallying cry.

You'll meet the qualities that set great entrepreneurs apart, like resilience, adaptability, and an unapologetic belief in your vision. You'll learn how to identify your own blind spots, build a team that has your back, and take advantage of the unique strengths that women bring to the table. Because let's be clear: we're not just capable of succeeding in the startup world—we're uniquely positioned to lead it into a better, more innovative future.

So why should you keep reading? Because this book isn't here to sugarcoat your entrepreneurial dreams. It's here to challenge you, to prepare you, and to give you the tools to face those challenges head-on. Whether you're still deciding if entrepreneurship is right for you or you're already knee-deep in building your business, this book will help you move forward with clarity, confidence, and maybe even a little humor to keep you sane.

Ladies, it's time to stop asking for permission and start demanding a seat at the table—or better yet, building our own tables. Let's rewrite the rules of business, one startup at a time.

You've got what it takes. Let's get to work.

Chapter 2: Personal Qualities of Failed Entrepreneurs

So, you want to be an entrepreneur? Fantastic! But before you dive headfirst into this world of pitch decks and late-night caffeine, there's something you need to know. Startups don't fail simply because their ideas are flawed, or because the market was fickle that year. No, one of the most common reasons is much closer to home: the personal qualities of the founder. That's right—many startups fall apart not because of the product or the plan, but because of the person behind it.

Consider this your friendly, albeit slightly bracing, warning. Certain personality traits—some of which we're about to detail—are almost surefire signs that your dream startup might hit the skids before it ever really leaves the ground. The good news? Recognizing these traits in yourself doesn't mean you're doomed. It means you have a chance to address them before they sink your ambitions.

If you see yourself in any of these qualities, you've got two options: work to develop the positive traits (the kind we'll explore in Chapter 3), or find a partner who fills in your blind spots. And honestly, pairing up can be a powerful move. It's common for one founder to be the "science" or "idea" person while the other founder brings the "people" skills, managerial savvy, or sales acumen. This dynamic duo often has a better shot at making it than a lone genius trying to do everything themselves. After all, attempting to build a business solo is a lot like trying to juggle flaming torches on a unicycle—it's not impossible, but burnout or disaster is practically guaranteed.

So, let's get into it, shall we? Here's a breakdown of the personal traits that, in my experience, are a recipe for entrepreneurial disaster. If any of these sound familiar, consider it a nudge toward self-reflection. It might save you from a world of trouble—and a lot of lost cash—down the line.

Lack of Passion and Drive

"Listen, I'll be straight with you. Building a startup is one of the toughest things you can do, and frankly, we look for founders who are borderline obsessed— someone who's been carrying this idea around like a favorite childhood toy, polishing it in their mind for years. If this is just a fleeting interest, a good idea

you cooked up last quarter, that's not enough to get you through the hard parts. The founders we back are the ones who have thought about their problem inside out, upside down, backwards, and forwards. They've been living with it, and they're convinced the world is incomplete without their solution. Obsession may sound extreme, but it's what fuels a founder through the countless late nights, the rejections, and the 2 a.m. pivot crises. Without that fire, I just don't see you getting over the inevitable walls you'll hit. So, for now, it's a pass from us." (said by every venture capitalist)

Indifference: Starting a business isn't something you can do half-heartedly, the way you might start a new fitness routine or pick up an old hobby. If you're not waking up each day with at least some flicker of excitement, that's a big red flag. Passion is what gets you through those long hours when the product isn't quite right, or the customers just aren't biting. It's the fire that keeps you going when every rational part of you wants to quit. Without it, it's all too easy to lose motivation when things get tough—which, spoiler alert, they absolutely will.

Fear of Failure: Here's the thing about entrepreneurship—it's an arena of big wins and even bigger risks. If you're paralyzed by the mere thought of failing, you might find yourself hesitating at every critical juncture, too afraid to make the moves that could propel you forward. Ironically, this fear can actually lead to the very failure you're so keen to avoid. The best entrepreneurs learn to make friends with the possibility of failure. They understand it's a teacher, not an executioner.

Accepting Stereotypes as Truth

One of the quickest ways to sabotage your entrepreneurial journey is internalizing the stereotypes that the business world throws at women. If you believe, even subconsciously, that you're less competent, less capable, or less deserving than your male counterparts, those beliefs can seep into your decisions, eroding your confidence and holding you back. Remember: the only person who can define your potential is you.

Overly Self-Critical

It's common for women entrepreneurs to hold themselves to impossibly high standards, often fueled by societal pressures to "do it all" perfectly. This self-criticism can lead to paralysis, hesitation, or burnout. Striving for excellence is great, but perfectionism can be a trap that stops you from taking bold, decisive action.

Avoiding Conflict

Women are often socialized to be agreeable and avoid confrontation, but in the startup world, avoiding conflict can mean failing to advocate for yourself or your business. Whether it's pushing back against an investor's lowball offer, negotiating fair terms with a partner, or addressing underperformance in your team, avoiding conflict often leads to unresolved issues that snowball over time.

Reluctance to Self-Promote

Let's be honest: many women are uncomfortable with self-promotion, fearing they'll come across as "braggy" or "arrogant." But if you can't confidently talk about your achievements, you're doing your business a disservice. Investors, customers, and potential partners need to hear why you and your startup are worth their attention.

Underestimating Financial Worth

Women founders often undervalue their companies or ask for less funding than they need. Whether it's negotiating an equity stake or pitching for investment, undervaluing your business (or yourself) can lead to underfunding, weaker partnerships, and slower growth. You're building something valuable—don't be afraid to ask for what it's worth.

Poor Decision-Making Skills

<u>Impulsiveness:</u> Now, quick decision-making can be a superpower in the startup world, but only if you have the right balance. Impulsiveness—acting without fully understanding or analyzing the consequences—often leads to expensive, time-consuming mistakes. Imagine a founder who decides to change the entire business model overnight, only to realize a few weeks later that the change alienated half their customer base. That's a costly error and one that could have been avoided with a little extra thought.

Indecisiveness: On the other side of the coin, there's indecisiveness, the art of waiting until every possible opportunity has faded into the rearview mirror. If you find yourself in a constant loop of weighing pros and cons, unable to pull the trigger, it's a serious handicap. Startup life moves fast. Sometimes, you need to make decisions on the fly—even if all the information isn't there. Waiting too long can mean you miss the window altogether.

Inability to Adapt

Rigidity: The startup world doesn't hand out awards for stubbornly clinging to your initial idea, especially when the market is screaming for something different. Rigidity—the refusal to adapt, even when all signs point to change—is a recipe for becoming obsolete. An unwillingness to pivot when needed has been the downfall of many a founder. Markets shift, technologies advance and customer preferences evolve—flexibility is the name of the game.

Resistance to Feedback: Constructive criticism is often the best (and cheapest) tool for growth, but founders who are closed off to feedback shut themselves off from invaluable insights. Think of feedback as free consulting; ignoring it not only stifles progress but can also alienate employees, customers, and investors. It's a surefire way to end up steering a ship that's veering dangerously off course.

Poor Financial Management

Overspending: Ah, the siren song of flashy office spaces, the latest tech gear, and maybe a few luxurious lunches. Many startups have floundered under the weight of their founders' lavish spending habits. Overspending without a realistic budget or a clear financial plan is like trying to fill a bathtub with a sieve. Eventually, the money runs out, and so does your runway.

Neglecting Financial Planning: "We'll figure it out as we go!" might sound adventurous, but in reality, winging it with your finances is a near-certain route to an early shutdown. Financial planning is essential, even if the numbers seem bleak in the beginning. Without a budget and a basic understanding of your cash flow, expenses will quickly outweigh revenue, leaving your startup in the red.

Lack of People Skills

<u>Inability to Ask for Investment Money:</u> Getting a business off the ground isn't cheap, and sooner or later, you'll need to ask for funding. But if you're uncomfortable or unprepared to approach investors, you're limiting your potential from the outset. This isn't the place to be shy—learning to confidently present your vision and request financial backing is a must.

<u>Inability to Network Effectively:</u> Networking isn't just for your LinkedIn profile; it's a lifeline. The people you meet can open doors to new partnerships, funding opportunities, or mentorships. If you're uncomfortable networking, you're potentially missing out on these vital connections.

<u>Poor Communication:</u> Communication skills may not sound as flashy as coding or negotiating, but they're foundational. Being able to clearly express your goals, expectations, and values to employees, investors, and customers alike is essential. Miscommunication can breed confusion, which, in turn, breeds frustration and setbacks.

<u>Inability to Build a Team:</u> Even the best ideas need a strong team to back them up. If you can't inspire or retain talent, your startup's growth will be stunted. Building a team isn't just about hiring people; it's

about finding people who share your vision and are willing to stick around through thick and thin.

Arrogance and Ego

<u>Overconfidence:</u> Confidence is good, but overconfidence—the kind that blinds you to your own limitations—can be fatal. If you think you know it all, you're probably overlooking critical flaws. An open mind and a willingness to learn are far more valuable in the long run than a bravado-filled façade.

<u>Disregard for Others:</u> Entrepreneurship isn't a solo endeavor. You need customers, employees, partners, and investors—all of whom deserve respect. If you lack empathy or ignore the needs of others, you'll soon find yourself in a lonely corner, and not a profitable one.

Procrastination

<u>Delaying Action:</u> Deadlines aren't just for paperwork; they're the fuel that keeps a startup moving forward. If you're a chronic procrastinator, putting off important tasks until the last minute, you'll miss out on countless opportunities and leave important details neglected.

<u>Fear of the Unknown:</u> Growth comes from tackling the unfamiliar, yet the fear of venturing into the unknown keeps many entrepreneurs anchored to the same old routines. If you shy away from new challenges, your business will never reach its full potential.

In summary, being aware of these traits doesn't spell certain doom; it's simply the first step in avoiding potential pitfalls. Consider this list your personal roadmap to success, a guide to recognize and shed what doesn't serve you. Entrepreneurship demands a willingness to adapt, to seek feedback, to listen, and, most of all, to grow. Embracing those challenges now can give you a fighting chance when the going gets tough.

Chapter 3: Personal Qualities of Successful Entrepreneurs

So, you've braved Chapter 2's dark corridor of startup warning signs and personal foibles, and you're still here. Congratulations! That's already a promising start. Now, let's shift gears and focus on the traits that fuel success—the qualities that distinguish those rare entrepreneurs who rise above the chaos, confusion, and caffeine overdoses to build something extraordinary. While business plans and market strategies are all good, they're no match for the right mindset.

No single personality trait guarantees success, of course, but a blend of the qualities we're about to explore can give you a solid leg up. And no, this isn't some pep talk about "believing in yourself." Real entrepreneurship calls for more than blind optimism—it calls for grit, flexibility, a good dose of humility, and a willingness to roll up your sleeves. Let's dive in.

Professional Behavior

Elizabeth Holmes' early success stemmed from her ability to craft a compelling vision, exude unwavering professionalism and confidence, look people directly in the eye, and convince investors of her serious abilities with a charismatic narrative. Even the savviest of them stood in line to give her millions in funding. She positioned herself as a trailblazing female entrepreneur in a male-dominated industry. Holmes focused on projecting credibility through her deep voice, steady gaze, scant attention to hair and makeup, Steve Jobs-inspired black wardrobe, and promises of revolutionary innovation. However, she failed to produce on her claims and ended up in jail because in her drive to live up to her image, she also faked reports of her company's performance. Don't fabricate performance, but emulate everything else.

I tell my female clients to cultivate a super professional image like Elizabeth Holmes', without the fraud. Nobody wants to invest millions of dollars in a giggly, flirty girl in a pink Barbie dress. Wear a black suit and keep the makeup minimal. Be serious in your demeanor and use proper English. No obvious flirting beyond being charming. You aren't looking to find a boyfriend, And you will have plenty of men trying to get in your pants for the manly challenge of it. You don't want a reputation for anything other than your intelligence and your brilliant startup idea. You want to look reliable and smart, not cool.

Confidence in Breaking the Mold

Successful women entrepreneurs aren't afraid to challenge societal expectations. Whether it's leading a male-dominated team, entering a "non-traditional" industry, or shaking up traditional business models, they embrace the unique perspectives and strengths that come with being a woman in business. Confidence in your individuality can be your superpower.

Patience in the Face of Bias

Unfortunately, bias is a reality for many women entrepreneurs. Successful founders don't let it define them. Instead, they develop a thick skin, learning to navigate microaggressions, dismissive attitudes, or double standards without losing focus or self-worth. Resilience doesn't mean ignoring bias—it means refusing to let it stop you.

Strategic Relationship Building

Women entrepreneurs often excel at cultivating meaningful, supportive relationships, and this trait can be a huge advantage. If romance happens, make sure it's real and reliable. You don't want a vengeful lover or a jerk spreading rumors or compromising pictures of you as you are about to sign a funding deal. Successful founders leverage relationship skill to build strong networks, foster collaborations, and create communities of allies who champion their businesses.

Clear Boundry Setting

In a world that often expects women to be endlessly accommodating, successful entrepreneurs know how to set boundaries. Whether it's managing client demands, balancing personal and professional life, or avoiding burnout, they protect their time and energy, ensuring they can give their best to their business.

Advocacy for Women in Business

The best women entrepreneurs understand that lifting others up doesn't detract from their success—it amplifies it. They mentor other women, advocate for gender equity in their industries, and work to create opportunities for the next generation of women leaders. Empowering others is a powerful part of their legacy.

Passion and Drive

This is the beating heart of entrepreneurship. Passion is more than mere enthusiasm; it's the fuel that powers you through late nights, uncertain outcomes, and endless obstacles. A deep-seated love for what you're doing gives you the stamina to keep going when others might throw in the towel. True passion isn't swayed by bad days, market fluctuations, or the occasional existential crisis. It's relentless, and it's the engine that keeps your startup alive long after the novelty has worn off.

Teachability

Think you know everything? Then entrepreneurship might not be for you. The best founders are sponges—they absorb knowledge from anyone and everyone, from mentors and investors to customers and competitors. Teachability means not just asking for advice but truly listening to it. It's a willingness to pivot based on feedback, learn from mistakes, and constantly improve. Teachability is the antidote to arrogance, keeping you open to new perspectives that might be the key to your next breakthrough.

Resilience

Entrepreneurship isn't for the faint-hearted; setbacks are part of the game. Resilience is the ability to absorb failure, recalibrate, and keep moving forward. Every entrepreneur will face rejections, missed opportunities, and occasional disasters—what sets the successful ones apart is their capacity to bounce back, often stronger than before. In many ways, resilience is more critical than initial success, because startups rarely follow a straight path to glory. It's a winding road, and resilience is your best companion on the journey.

Risk Tolerance

If the thought of taking a risk makes you break out in hives, entrepreneurship might feel a bit like a haunted house—thrilling but perhaps too terrifying to enjoy. Successful entrepreneurs embrace risk as part of the process. They don't take wild gambles, mind you, but they do make calculated decisions that push the boundaries. They step outside their comfort zones regularly, and they know that failure isn't fatal. Risk is an integral part of building something new, and the ability to tolerate and even welcome it is a hallmark of the entrepreneurial mindset.

Adaptability

Market conditions change, customers are fickle, and competition is ruthless. In the face of such unpredictability, adaptability is essential. This quality allows entrepreneurs to pivot when their original plan goes off-course. Successful founders aren't wed to any single vision or approach; instead, they treat their business like an evolving organism, adjusting and improving as circumstances demand. Adaptability is what keeps you relevant, giving you a long-term shot in a world that never stands still.

Creativity and Innovation

Problem-solving is at the core of every startup, and creativity is what brings it to life. Innovation isn't always about inventing the next smartphone; often, it's about finding clever, efficient solutions to everyday challenges. Entrepreneurs with a creative streak think outside the box, approaching obstacles with fresh perspectives that turn roadblocks into opportunities. They look at problems differently, and that uniqueness often becomes their competitive advantage.

Strong Work Ethic

For all the myths about flexible schedules and endless leisure time, entrepreneurship is anything but an easy ride. Building a company requires stamina, dedication, and a readiness to dive into the grind. Entrepreneurs who succeed know that hard work isn't optional; it's a given. They're willing to put in the hours, often sacrificing short-term comforts for long-term gains. If you're hoping for a nine-to-five, this probably isn't the field for you.

Leadership Skills

A successful entrepreneur is also a capable leader, someone who can inspire a team, rally support, and bring out the best in others. Leadership isn't just about barking orders or putting on a confident front—it's about setting a vision and guiding people toward it, knowing when to delegate, and showing genuine appreciation for the contributions of others. Many women think that in order to appear capable and in charge, they must act like bitches. They're unpleasant to work with and such behavior tends to result in mistakes. A good leader creates a culture of trust and collaboration, and that's the foundation on which great companies are built.

Effective Communication

Clear, persuasive communication is the backbone of a thriving business. Whether you're pitching to investors, inspiring employees, or engaging customers, how you articulate your vision matters immensely. Communication isn't just about talking; it's about listening, too. Successful entrepreneurs know how to convey their ideas succinctly, understand others' needs, and create dialogues that drive the business forward. It's also important not to be too confidential regarding your business operations or your personal life. If you can't communicate effectively, you'll find it tough to gain support or convey the value of what you're building.

Financial Acumen

Yes, even the most visionary entrepreneurs need to know how to handle money. Financial acumen doesn't mean you have to be a math whiz or a CPA, but you should have a solid grasp of budgeting, forecasting, and cash flow. Money is the lifeblood of a startup, and poor financial decisions can be the nail in its coffin. Entrepreneurs who understand financial basics are far better equipped to make informed decisions, ensuring that their ideas don't run out of fuel too soon.

Self-Belief

If you don't believe in yourself, who will? A strong sense of self-belief is the spark that lights the fire of every successful entrepreneur. This isn't blind optimism but a steady conviction in your abilities and the potential of your idea. Self-belief gives you the courage to push forward when everyone else thinks you're crazy. It's the secret ingredient that helps you weather the storms and keep your eyes fixed on the horizon, even when the path ahead is anything but certain.

Unapologetic Ambition

Successful women founders don't downplay their ambitions, just to make others comfortable. They set bold goals, dream big, and pursue success unapologetically. Ambition, when paired with hard work and strategic thinking, is a key driver of their achievements.

The Big Picture

These qualities, while invaluable, aren't a guarantee of success. Every entrepreneur's journey is unique, and success often depends on a blend of personality traits, timing, and a bit of good fortune. The startup world isn't a "one-size-fits-all" scenario; it's a custom-made rollercoaster that'll test your limits in ways you can't predict. And, just as importantly, the journey will reveal strengths and skills you might not even know you had.

So if you see these qualities in yourself, take it as a good sign. Keep refining them, keep learning, and keep pushing forward. These traits are the tools in your entrepreneurial toolkit—the qualities that will help you adapt, innovate, and lead. And remember, no one arrives fully formed; successful entrepreneurs are works in progress. The key is to stay open, stay driven, and let the journey itself shape you into the entrepreneur you're meant to become.

Chapter 4 dives deeper into each stage with more insights, examples, and practical advice for you budding entrepreneurs.

Chapter 4: From Idea to Launch

So, you've got an idea—a gleaming, revolutionary concept that's destined to disrupt an industry, send your competitors scrambling, and ideally make you rich in the process. Maybe it's a new piece of wearable tech, an app that can anticipate needs before you know you have them, or a system so efficient it'll put your competitors out of business. Whatever your idea, it's probably still swirling around in your head, ambitious and untested.

But here's the reality: an idea alone doesn't make a business. In fact, most ideas don't get anywhere near the finish line. Why? Because turning that "lightbulb moment" into a full-fledged company takes more than inspiration; it takes grit, resilience, some financial know-how, and—perhaps most importantly—a plan.

Let's dig into what it actually takes to move from concept to launch, breaking down each step and offering the kind of real-talk advice that might just save you some time, money, and sanity.

The Idea: The Foundation of Your Business

First things first: let's talk about your idea. Aspiring entrepreneurs often get hung up on having a "cool" product or a flashy app, something that seems novel at first glance. But a truly viable startup idea isn't just cool—it's necessary. It solves a real problem or provides value that customers are missing. If your concept doesn't make life easier, faster, or more enjoyable in some fundamental way, it may not gain traction. The best startup ideas are those that, once realized, make people wonder how they ever lived without them.

To put it simply, the idea isn't just about what's possible but what's practical. Is there room for it in the market? And does it meet a genuine need? If the answer to either question is shaky, don't despair—consider it a chance to refine your concept before moving ahead.

Market Fit: Will They Actually Pay for This?

You're sold on your idea, but are your customers? The concept of "market fit" is crucial: it's the answer to whether people will actually spend money on what you're offering. Many budding entrepreneurs assume that if they find it valuable, others will, too. But in reality, the process of discovering market fit is a lot more nuanced and requires real research.

Think of market fit as a test of your idea's staying power. Conduct surveys, talk to potential customers, run focus groups—do whatever it takes to gather feedback and understand your target audience. Is there a genuine demand for your product? Would people use it regularly, or is it more of a one-off novelty? And, importantly, will they pay what you need to charge to keep your business afloat?

Don't cut corners here. A failure to truly understand your market is why so many startups end up as expensive lessons rather than success stories. Your friends and family might love the concept, but unless you're planning to open a business exclusively for them, you'll need a broader audience's buy-in.

Production: From Prototype to Product

So, you've got a solid idea, and you've confirmed that there's a market out there. Now, how will you bring it to life? Production is the stage where your idea turns into something tangible, whether that's a physical product, an app, or a service. But as straightforward as that sounds, production can be a labyrinth of cost estimates, logistical hurdles, and timing setbacks.

If your product requires complex manufacturing, you'll need to factor in everything from raw materials and equipment to labor and quality control. For tech startups, production might involve months (or years) of coding, testing, and debugging before you have something market-ready. Every layer of complexity adds cost, and each step forward is a new opportunity to spend money you might not have yet. So, keep your production plans realistic and adaptable, and always build in room for unexpected expenses or delays.

Funding: Fuel for the Startup Engine

Ah, funding—the lifeblood of any startup. Once you've got a business plan and a rough estimate of production costs, you'll need to raise money to make it happen. Depending on your startup's nature and scope, you might need anywhere from a few thousand to a few million dollars to get things off the ground. Let's break down the typical stages of startup funding:

Friends & Family Round: This is often where the initial funds come from—your personal network. A "friends and family" round typically raises up to $250,000 and is used to cover foundational costs like legal fees, early-stage marketing, and branding. But this money comes with a word of caution: mixing personal relationships with business can be risky, so be clear about terms and manage expectations carefully. This round is also where many startups get their first test of "buy-in," gauging how strongly others believe in their idea.

Angel Investors: Angel investors are high-net-worth individuals with a taste for risky ventures and a soft spot for startups. Angels are often willing to invest up to $1 million if they believe in your concept. What makes them unique is that they're typically more interested in you—the founder—than in your company's immediate revenue potential. They're investing in your vision, your plan, and your potential to bring it to life, so be prepared to sell them on more than just your idea.

Venture Capital (VC): This is the big league, where larger sums of money are on the line, and VCs don't just hand out checks lightly. Venture capitalists invest in companies with proven demand and high-growth potential. They're looking for serious returns, so unless you have a viable product and some early traction, you may not be VC-ready. VCs come with high expectations and stringent oversight, but for companies ready to scale, VC funding can provide the resources and credibility needed to make a splash.

Networking: Turning Connections into Opportunities

Networking is essential in the startup world, but it's often a misunderstood art. To many founders, networking means hitting up industry events, swapping business cards, or trying to get investors to follow them back on LinkedIn. In reality, networking is also about building meaningful relationships. It's about connecting with people who can help you, advise you, and sometimes even open doors you didn't know existed.

Start small by reaching out to other founders, investors, or even friends in related industries. Attend events, sign up for industry-specific groups, and don't be afraid to follow up after that first introduction. Remember, it's not about collecting contacts; it's about building a support network that can help you through the inevitable ups and downs of startup life.

Build-Out: Making a Game Plan

Launching a startup without a game plan is like trying to run a marathon without knowing the course. A solid business plan is your map—it lays out your destination, your path, and the markers you'll use to check your progress. This plan should cover your timeline, budget, milestones, and key goals. Investors will want to see this, of course, but more importantly, *you* need it to stay on track. Consider it your accountability partner as you move from idea to execution.

Building a startup requires juggling many roles, from visionary to project manager to accountant, and without a clear plan, it's all too easy to lose focus. A good business plan helps you prioritize, ensuring that each decision moves you closer to your end goal.

Legal: Setting Up Your Business Right

Let's face it: legal paperwork probably isn't what got you excited about starting a business. However, establishing a legal entity (a corporation, LLC, etc.) and drawing up clear agreements with partners, investors, and early employees is crucial. You'll need bank accounts, investment paperwork, intellectual property protection, and more. Think of this stage as building a strong foundation—without it, your business will be on shaky ground from the start.

Accounting: Show Me the Money Management

Even if your startup is barely scraping by, accounting is a must. From day one, track every dollar coming in and going out. Get a good accounting software, set up a budget, and use it religiously. Not only will this help you make better financial decisions, but it will also prove invaluable when you pitch to investors. They want to see a startup that takes financial management seriously—messy books and ambiguous spending are red flags that suggest a lack of foresight and responsibility.

Compliance: Navigating the Red Tape

Compliance might sound like a bureaucratic headache, but in regulated industries—healthcare, finance, or even tech—it's a non-negotiable. Every industry has rules and standards that businesses must follow, and ignoring these can lead to legal trouble or financial penalties. Compliance isn't just about avoiding fines; it's about demonstrating to customers and investors alike that your business is trustworthy and professional.

Putting It All Together

Turning an idea into a real, functioning business is a bit like putting together a puzzle where the pieces keep shifting. You'll need to balance creativity with caution, risk-taking with strategic planning, and ambition with a grounded understanding of the practical challenges ahead.

Consider each section of this chapter a step in your roadmap from dream to reality. Yes, it's a daunting process, and yes, there will be times when you feel in over your head. But every entrepreneur who's made it through the launch process knows that each challenge is a chance to learn, grow, and refine the vision that inspired them in the first place.

Launching a startup is as exhilarating as it is exhausting, and if you've made it this far, you're already showing the kind of dedication that sets successful founders apart. Remember, your idea is just the beginning—the journey of transforming it into a thriving business is where the real adventure lies.

Chapter 5: Advice

The Challenges of Being a Woman Entrepreneur
 (to be added to Chapter 4 or 5, wherever it fits best)

So, let's address the elephant in the room: being a woman in the startup world isn't just about building a business—it's also about navigating a landscape that, let's face it, isn't always designed with us in mind.

Male-dominated boardrooms, mansplaining investors, and a persistent (if unspoken) assumption that women can't "do math" or "handle pressure"— these are just a few of the joys awaiting female entrepreneurs. It's not just outdated stereotypes; the numbers back it up. Women founders receive less than 3% of venture capital funding globally. Let that sink in. It means that no matter how brilliant your pitch deck is, you might find yourself fighting twice as hard for half the recognition (or funding) of your male counterparts.

But don't let this dishearten you. Let it fire you up.

Navigating the Double Standards

There's a frustrating paradox that women founders

often encounter. You're expected to prove your competence twice over, but if you're too confident, you're labeled "arrogant" or "unlikeable." Investors might ask if you plan on having kids, while your male counterparts get grilled about their five-year growth projections. The double standard is real, and it's exhausting, but the good news is that awareness of these biases is growing. More women-focused investor networks and mentorship programs are emerging to level the playing field. Seek them out—they can be a game-changer.

Finding Allies (and Advocates)

Another challenge women face is the lack of tailored advice. While male founders often have mentors or "boys' club" connections to guide them, women are often left figuring it out on their own. That's where building your own network comes in. Look for women-led incubators, accelerators, and networking groups that can offer resources, support, and yes, introductions to the right investors. And don't shy away from male allies—they exist, and many are genuinely eager to help level the playing field.

Reclaiming Confidence

One of the toughest hurdles for many women entrepreneurs is battling impostor syndrome. It's not just a personal struggle; it's reinforced by a culture that still, in some corners, questions women's intelligence and abilities. But here's the secret: your value as a founder isn't determined by anyone else's opinion. You've done the work. You've built the idea. You belong in this space.

When you're pitching your idea or negotiating a deal, speak with confidence—not just for yourself, but for the women who will come after you. Every time you break through a barrier, you're paving the way for the next generation of women entrepreneurs.

Changing the Narrative

The world of entrepreneurship is changing. Slowly, yes, but it's changing. With every woman who secures funding, builds a successful startup, or proves the naysayers wrong, the narrative shifts. You're not just building a business—you're challenging a system that has, for too long, underestimated half the population.

So, yes, the road is harder for us. But it's also more rewarding. Because when we succeed, it's not just a win for our businesses; it's a win for every woman who dreams of following in our footsteps.

Keep going. Keep building. And remember: the system isn't stacked against you because you're incapable—it's stacked against you because it's terrified of your potential. Show them what you're made of.

So, you're ready to launch your startup. You've got the idea, the plan, and maybe even a rough sketch of your logo, all ready to go. But before you jump into the deep end, let's pause for a moment of real talk. Starting a business is hard. *Really* hard. It's a journey that will test every ounce of your patience, creativity, and determination. Forget the glamorized stories of self-made billionaires jetting around in private planes; the reality for most entrepreneurs looks more like sleepless nights, bank accounts that hover dangerously close to zero, and more rejections than you ever dreamed possible.

Consider this chapter your pep talk mixed with a dose of practicality. Here's some advice to help you navigate the wild waters of the startup world with a few less bruises and a bit more perspective.

Forget the Stories of Overnight Wealth

The tech billionaire in the news? The one who "made it big" with what seemed like an effortless, meteoric rise? Chances are, they didn't. What the headlines don't show you is that they likely spent years living out of their car, couch-surfing, or surviving off instant noodles. Stories of overnight success sell newspapers, but they're far from the norm. For most entrepreneurs, the path to success is anything but glamorous. It's late nights, high stress, and a few financial scrapes along the way.

If you're jumping into the startup world with visions of overnight wealth, you're in for a rough wake-up call. Building a business takes time, patience, and a willingness to keep going long after the initial excitement has faded. Focus less on the headlines and more on building something meaningful; if wealth follows, consider it a happy side effect of your dedication.

Don't Go It Alone

If there's one lesson I can't stress enough, it's this: *You can't do it all by yourself.* Founding a startup is a monumental task, and even the most brilliant founders find themselves overwhelmed by the sheer amount of work. This is where a co-founder can be invaluable. A co-founder brings another perspective, different skills, and most importantly, someone to share the load. And trust me, there will be days when having someone by your side makes all the difference between pushing forward and throwing in the towel.

When choosing a co-founder, look for someone who complements your strengths and fills in your weaknesses. If you're the "idea" person, maybe they're the one with the financial savvy or the managerial know-how. A good co-founder can be the support system you need to keep going when the going gets tough, and they're worth their weight in gold.

Seek Out Advisors (Yes, Even Your Uncle Joe)

No matter how much you think you know, there's always more to learn. Advisors bring expertise, perspective, and often, a much-needed reality check.

If you have a relative or family friend who's started a business, reach out—they may have insights that could save you time and money, or even spare you from a major pitfall. Many entrepreneurs think they have to reinvent the wheel, but the truth is, there's a lot to be gained from learning from others' experiences.

Advisors can come from all walks of life—business owners, professors, industry veterans, and even former competitors. Be open-minded and willing to listen. You don't have to follow every piece of advice, but having multiple perspectives helps you make better-informed decisions.

Save Up—You'll Need It

One of the least glamorous but most important pieces of advice I can offer: "save your money". It might sound dull, but building a business requires capital—often more than you initially think. From legal fees and accounting to marketing and consulting, there's a long list of expenses you'll need to cover, and those costs add up quickly. The more you can save before launching, the less stress you'll feel when your expenses start rolling in.

Start setting aside funds now, even if your launch date is months or years away. Every dollar saved is one less dollar you'll have to scrounge up later when the financial pinch really sets in. Think of it as an investment in your future, one that will give you a little more breathing room to focus on building your business rather than constantly worrying about bills.

Consider a Startup Accelerator

If you're looking for guidance, funding, and a crash course in startup life, a startup accelerator could be worth considering. These programs are designed to fast-track promising ideas, offering mentorship, resources, and sometimes funding in exchange for a small equity stake in your company. However, they're not a free pass—most accelerators have rigorous application processes, and they're not cheap. Some require a relocation to a different city for a few months, which means uprooting your life temporarily.

But for those willing to make the commitment, an accelerator can be a game-changer. You'll get direct feedback from industry experts, a structured environment to work on your business, and a network of peers facing similar challenges. Just keep in mind, that not all accelerators are created equal, so research carefully before committing to one. And remember, if you're not accepted, it doesn't mean your idea isn't worth pursuing—it just might need more refinement.

Get Ready for Rejection (Lots of It)

Brace yourself: in the world of startups, rejection is almost a rite of passage. You'll pitch to hundreds of potential investors, and it's very likely that 199 of them will turn you down. Investors will ask if you have revenues yet, if there's traction, if there's a massive customer base already clamoring for your product. They'll have all sorts of reasons for saying no, but here's the good news—*you only need one yes*. That's right, all it takes is one investor to believe in your vision, and everything changes.

The secret here is resilience. Rejections can feel deeply personal, but they're often not a reflection on you or your idea—they're simply a mismatch of timing, focus, or funding priorities. Every "no" brings you one step closer to that crucial "yes." So keep pitching, keep refining, and don't let rejection deter you. Resilience, perhaps more than anything else, is what separates those who succeed from those who give up.

Embrace a Lean Mindset

In the startup world, efficiency is everything. Forget about fancy office spaces or extravagant launch parties. The best entrepreneurs know that lean operations are the key to survival in the early stages. Focus on the essentials, and cut out anything that doesn't directly contribute to your growth. Be ruthless about prioritizing what truly matters, and don't get distracted by what *looks* impressive.

A lean mindset isn't just about budgeting, though; it's about adaptability. In a startup, things rarely go exactly as planned, and a lean approach lets you pivot quickly when necessary. When you keep your operations efficient, you're better able to respond to the unexpected and stay focused on your goals without getting bogged down by unnecessary costs.

Keep Learning and Adapting

The startup journey is a continuous learning process. Stay curious, read widely, and keep up with industry trends. Learn from competitors, but also from businesses outside your field. Every new skill you pick up, every piece of knowledge you acquire, makes you better equipped to handle the challenges ahead. Remember, there's no such thing as a static business model; you'll need to adapt constantly, and staying informed is the best way to be ready.

Consider taking courses in areas where you're less confident—whether that's coding, marketing, or finance. The startup world changes fast, and staying sharp gives you a better chance to navigate those changes successfully.

Final Thoughts: The Real Work Begins Now

Starting a business is a leap of faith, an adventure filled with challenges, setbacks, and unexpected detours. It's easy to get swept up in the excitement of having a brilliant idea, but it's the hard work, resilience, and dedication that truly make or break a startup.

Take this advice as a foundation, a reminder that success in the startup world isn't handed to anyone. It's earned through persistence, adaptability, and a willingness to roll with the punches. And while the road is tough, the reward of seeing your idea take flight is one of the most fulfilling experiences out there.

In the end, remember: the journey of entrepreneurship is as important as the destination. So buckle up, stay focused, and enjoy the ride. After all, you're in for an experience that few others are brave enough to attempt.

Conclusion: The Journey Ahead

Congratulations on making it to the end of this book! If you've come this far, it's safe to say that you're serious about the entrepreneurial journey. You've read about the grit, resilience, and adaptability needed to build a startup, from the initial spark of an idea to the many hurdles of the launch process, and everything in between. By now, you know that entrepreneurship isn't just about the glitz and glamour of creating something new; it's a demanding path, filled with unpredictable turns, long nights, and countless decisions. But for those with the right mindset, it's also one of the most rewarding challenges you'll ever take on.

Starting a business is never a straight line, and each entrepreneur's journey is unique. There will be moments of pure exhilaration—like the first time you see someone using your product or the day you land that critical investment. There will also be moments of doubt when it feels like nothing is going right and you question if you made the right decision. These ups and downs aren't just part of the journey; they *are* the journey. Each success and setback, each "yes" and "no," will shape you into the entrepreneur you're meant to become.

If there's one lasting takeaway from this book, let it be this: stay open, stay curious, and stay determined. There's no single formula for success in the startup world; there's only your path, your choices, and your willingness to keep moving forward, no matter how challenging it may seem. Success may not come overnight, but with resilience and a genuine passion for what you're building, it *will* come. Remember, every successful entrepreneur started right where you are now—with an idea, a bit of courage, and a whole lot of uncertainty. What makes the difference is a commitment to learning, adapting, and growing along the way.

And as you navigate the world of entrepreneurship, know that you're not alone. Reach out to mentors, seek out advice, and connect with others who share your journey. Surround yourself with people who believe in your vision, but don't be afraid of constructive criticism either—it's one of the most valuable tools you have for improvement. Embrace learning, even when it means admitting you're not the expert, and stay humble enough to recognize that each day offers a new lesson.

Now, as you close this book and take your first steps (or next steps) as an entrepreneur, I hope you'll keep the advice within these pages close at hand. The journey won't be easy, but that's part of what makes it meaningful. There's something extraordinary about creating something from nothing, about transforming an idea into a reality that changes lives, even if only in small ways. The world needs people like you—those willing to take risks, to solve problems, and to pursue dreams that others might not even imagine.

One last favor before we part ways: if you found this book helpful, inspiring, or even just entertaining, please consider leaving a positive review on Amazon. Your feedback not only helps other aspiring entrepreneurs find this book but also allows me to continue writing and refining these resources. Reviews are like a currency in the world of publishing, and your support means more than you know.

And if you know someone else who's thinking about starting their own venture or has that entrepreneurial spirit, pass along a recommendation. Share what you've learned here with friends, colleagues, or even that family member who's always brimming with ideas. You never know who might find the spark they need from something in these pages.

Thank you for taking this journey with me. Here's to the road ahead, to the highs and lows, the setbacks and triumphs, and to the incredible things you're about to create. Keep going, keep building, and never lose sight of why you started in the first place. The best is yet to come, and I, for one, can't wait to see what you'll accomplish.

> *Dreams ignite the flame,*
>
> *Barriers rise, yet she builds—*
>
> *Strength shapes her own path.*

References

Blank, S., & Dorf, B. (2012). The Startup Owner's Manual: The Step-By-Step Guide for Building a Great Company. K&S Ranch Publishing.

This book offers a hands-on, practical approach to starting a company, filled with insights on product-market fit, customer development, and business models.

Christensen, C. (1997). The Innovator's Dilemma: When New Technologies Cause Great Firms to Fail. Harvard Business Review Press.

Christensen's foundational work on disruptive innovation has influenced entrepreneurs and leaders, offering strategies to capitalize on market disruptions.

Ries, E. (2011). The Lean Startup: How Today's Entrepreneurs Use Continuous Innovation to Create Radically Successful Businesses. Crown Business.

A must-read for modern entrepreneurs, Ries explains the principles of the lean startup methodology, focusing on rapid iteration and customer feedback.

Sinek, S. (2009). *Start with Why: How Great Leaders Inspire Everyone to Take Action.* Portfolio.

Sinek's book explores the importance of purpose, arguing that successful companies and leaders start with a clear "why" to inspire growth and loyalty.

Thiel, P. (2014). *Zero to One: Notes on Startups, or How to Build the Future.* Crown Business.

Thiel shares insights on how to create unique value in competitive markets, encouraging entrepreneurs to innovate in ways that lead to true breakthroughs.

Aulet, B. (2013). *Disciplined Entrepreneurship: 24 Steps to a Successful Startup.* Wiley.

This step-by-step guide is based on MIT's entrepreneurship course and covers market segmentation, product development, and customer engagement.

Kawasaki, G. (2004). *The Art of the Start: The Time-Tested, Battle-Hardened Guide for Anyone Starting Anything.* Penguin Group.

Kawasaki's book provides actionable advice on launching, managing, and scaling a startup, emphasizing practical wisdom and an entrepreneurial attitude.

Osterwalder, A., & Pigneur, Y. (2010). Business Model Generation: A Handbook for Visionaries, Game Changers, and Challengers. Wiley.

This guide introduces the business model canvas, a strategic tool that helps entrepreneurs visualize and plan every aspect of their startup.

Knapp, J., Zeratsky, J., & Kowitz, B. (2016). Sprint: How to Solve Big Problems and Test New Ideas in Just Five Days. Simon & Schuster.

Based on Google Ventures' sprint process, this book offers a five-day framework for rapid prototyping and testing new ideas.

Gerber, M. E. (1995). The E-Myth Revisited: Why Most Small Businesses Don't Work and What to Do About It. Harper Business.

Gerber emphasizes the importance of systems and processes, warning against the "entrepreneurial myth" that passion alone can drive success.

Grit: The Power of Passion and Perseverance by Angela Duckworth (2016). Scribner.

Duckworth explores the concept of "grit" and how determination and resilience play critical roles in achieving long-term goals, including entrepreneurship.

Timmons, J. A., & Spinelli, S. (2009). New Venture Creation: Entrepreneurship for the 21st Century. McGraw-Hill Education.

This textbook provides comprehensive coverage on entrepreneurship, including financing, business models, and navigating startup challenges.

Harvard Business Review (Various Articles). Harvard Business Publishing.

Numerous HBR articles offer insights into entrepreneurship, leadership, innovation, and market strategy from experts across industries.

CB Insights. (2023). Why Startups Fail: A Post-Mortem Analysis. CB Insights Research.

A research report analyzing common reasons startups fail, with insights drawn from thousands of startup case studies and founder interviews.

U.S. Small Business Administration (SBA). (2023). Small Business Resource Guide.

The SBA provides resources and guides on small business finance, compliance, and legal structures, useful for startups in the U.S.

These resources cover a range of startup-related topics, from initial idea validation to scaling and managing growth. These references will provide readers with a foundation of resources for continued learning.

About the Author

Meet Victoria Duff:

With an impressive background in Wall Street investment banking and corporate finance spanning over two decades, Victoria brings a wealth of experience from working with Fortune 100 companies in the automobile, steel, oil, and banking sectors, as well as leading investment advisory firms and city funds. In 1997, she made the bold decision to step away from Wall Street and establish her own startup consultancy, aBusinessPlan.com. Throughout her career, Victoria has successfully overseen numerous friends and family rounds, crowdfunding, venture capital, and equity events, making her a seasoned expert in the field.

LinkedIn: https://www.linkedin.com/in/victoriaduff/

www.ingramcontent.com/pod-product-compliance
Lightning Source LLC
Chambersburg PA
CBHW071108240526